POPULAR SHEET
30 HITS FROM 2014-2016

MW00529388

ISBN 978-1-4950-6989-5

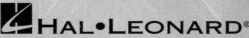

HAL•LEONARD®

7777 W. BLUEMOUND RD. P.O. BOX 13819 MILWAUKEE, WI 53213

Visit Hal Leonard Online at
www.halleonard.com

CONTENTS

ALL I ASK

Words and Music by ADELE ADKINS,
PHILIP LAWRENCE, BRUNO MARS
and CHRIS BROWN

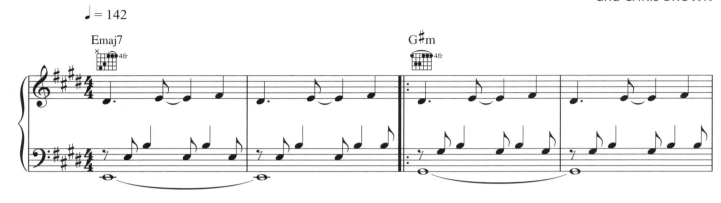

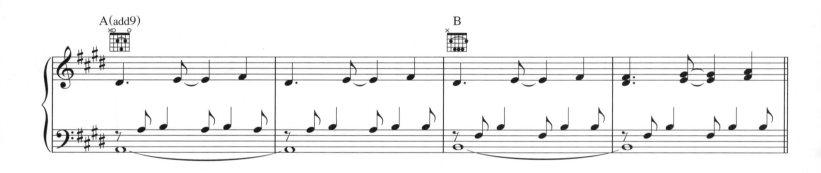

1. I will leave __ my heart at the door, __ I won't
2. I don't need __ your hon - es - ty, __ it's al - read - y in __

BUDAPEST

Words and Music by GEORGE BARNETT
and JOEL POTT

Moderately fast

My house in Bu - da - pest; my, ___ my hid - den treas - ure chest;

gold - en grand pi - an - o; ___ my beau - ti - ful cas - til - lo: you, ooh, ___

you, ooh, ___ I'd leave it all.

Ba - by, if you hold me then all ____ of this will go ____ a - way. ____

To Coda ⊕

D.S. al Coda
(take 2nd ending)

ALL OF ME

Words and Music by JOHN STEPHENS
and TOBY GAD

CAN'T FEEL MY FACE

Words and Music by ABEL TESFAYE,
MAX MARTIN, SAVAN KOTECHA,
PETER SVENSSON and ALI PAYAMI

EX'S & OH'S

Words and Music by TANNER SCHNEIDER
and DAVE BASSETT

FADED

Words and Music by ANDERS FROEN,
GUNNAR GREVE, JESPER BORGEN,
and ALAN WALKER

* *Recorded a half step higher.*

I'M NOT THE ONLY ONE

Words and Music by SAM SMITH
and JAMES NAPIER

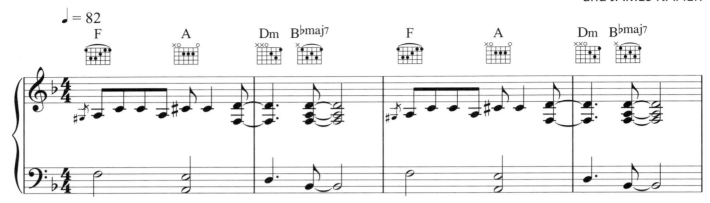

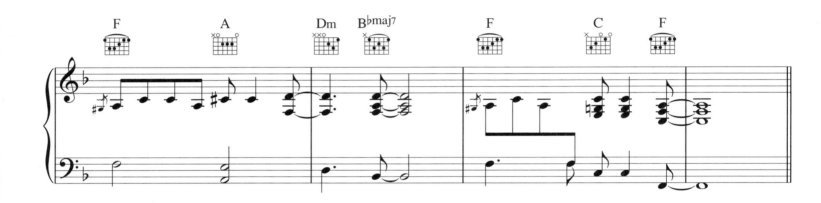

1. You and me, we made a vow   for bet-ter or for worse.

40

41

42

LET IT GO

Words and Music by JAMES BAY
and PAUL BARRY

* *Recorded a half step higher.*

LANTERNS

Words and Music by ADAM SPARK, IAN KENNY,
GLENN SARANGAPANY, IAN BERNEY
and ADAM WESTON

LET HER GO

Words and Music by
MICHAEL DAVID ROSENBERG

LOST BOY

Words and Music by
RUTH BERHE

Lyrics:

There was a time when I was a-lone, with no-where to go and no place to call home. My on-ly friend was The Man in the Moon, and e-ven some-times he would go a-way too. Then, one night as I

68

LOVE YOURSELF

Words and Music by JUSTIN BIEBER,
BENJAMIN LEVIN and ED SHEERAN

Moderate Ballad

MISS MOVIN' ON

Words and Music by JASON EVIGAN,
MITCH ALLAN, LINDY ROBBINS
and JULIA MICHAELS

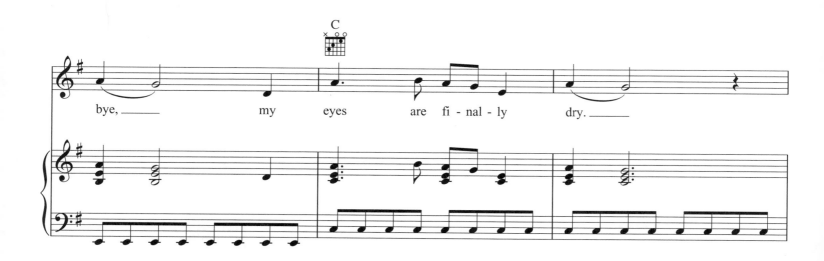

ONE CALL AWAY

Words and Music by CHARLIE PUTH,
BREYAN ISAAC, MATT PRIME,
JUSTIN FRANKS, BLAKE ANTHONY CARTER
and MAUREEN McDONALD

Recorded a half step higher.

OPHELIA

Words and Music by JEREMY FRAITES
and WESLEY SCHULTZ

RENEGADES

Words and Music by ALEXANDER JUNIOR GRANT,
ADAM LEVIN, CASEY HARRIS, NOAH FELDSHUH
and SAM HARRIS

RIPTIDE

Words and Music by
VANCE JOY

* Recorded a half step higher.

SAY SOMETHING

Words and Music by IAN AXEL,
CHAD VACCARINO and MIKE CAMPBELL

SEE YOU AGAIN

from FURIOUS 7

Words and Music by CAMERON THOMAZ,
CHARLIE PUTH, JUSTIN FRANKS
and ANDREW CEDAR

7 YEARS

Words and Music by LUKAS FORCHHAMMER,
MORTEN RISTORP, STEFAN FORREST,
DAVID LABREL, CHRISTOPHER BROWN
and MORTEN PILEGAARD

SHAKE IT OFF

Words and Music by TAYLOR SWIFT,
MAX MARTIN and SHELLBACK

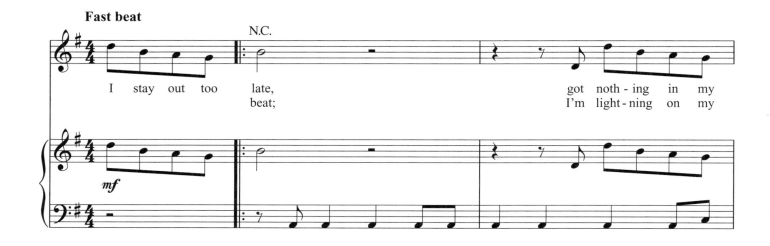

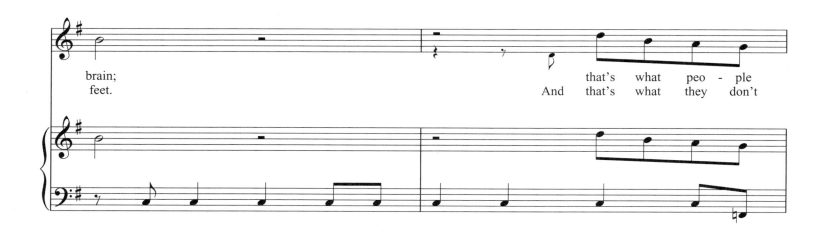

Additional Lyrics

Spoken: *Hey, hey, hey! Just think: While you've been getting*
Down and out about the liars and the dirty, dirty
Cheats of the world, you could've been getting down to
This. Sick. Beat!

Rap: My ex-man brought his new girlfriend.
She's like, "Oh, my god!" But I'm just gonna shake.
And to the fella over there with the hella good hair,
Won't you come on over, baby? We can shake, shake, shake.

SHAME

Words and Music by TYRESE GIBSON,
SAM DEES, RON KERSEY, WARREN CAMPBELL
and D.J. ROGERS, JR.

SHE USED TO BE MINE

Words and Music by
SARA BAREILLES

A SKY FULL OF STARS

Words and Music by GUY BERRYMAN,
JON BUCKLAND, WILL CHAMPION,
CHRIS MARTIN and TIM BERGLING

*Recorded a half step higher.

But I don't care _____ if you do, ____ ooh, ooh, __

ooh. _____ 'Cause in a sky, _____ 'cause in a

sky _____ full of stars, ___ I think I {saw / see} you. _____

To Coda ⊕

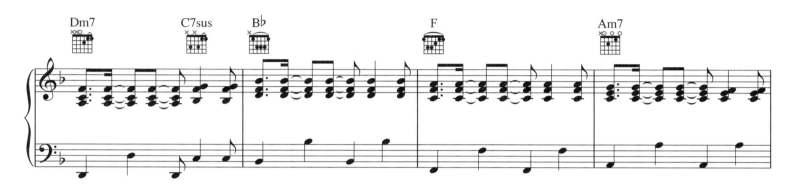

I think I see you.

You're such a heav - en - ly view.

STAND BY YOU

Words and Music by RACHEL PLATTEN,
JOY WILLIAMS, JACK ANTONOFF,
JON LEVINE and MATTHEW B. MORRIS

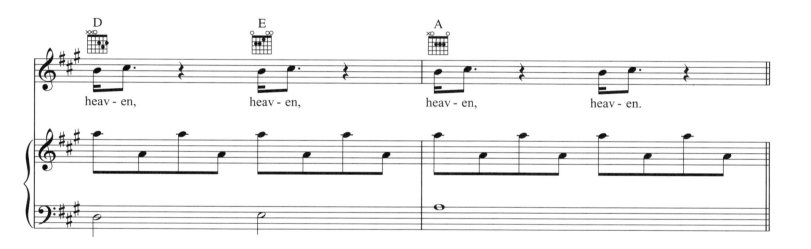

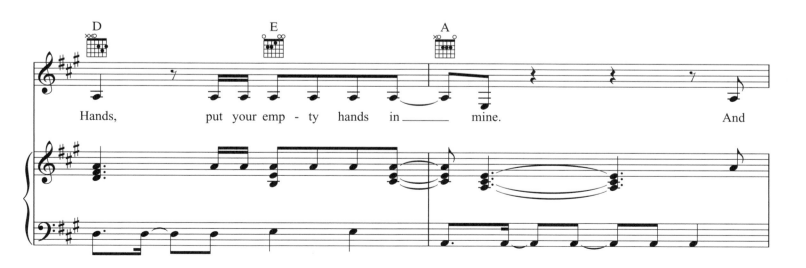

STITCHES

Words and Music by TEDDY GEIGER,
DANNY PARKER and DANIEL KYRIAKIDES

Recorded a half step lower.

TAKE ME TO CHURCH

Words and Music by
ANDREW HOZIER-BYRNE

Moderate Ballad

My lov-er's got hu-mour, she's the gig-gle at a fu-n'ral.

Knows ev-'ry-bod-y's dis-ap-prov-al, I should've wor-shipped her soon-er.

If the heav-ens ev-er did speak, she's the last __ true mouth-piece. Ev-'ry Sun-day's get-ting more bleak,

TEAR IN MY HEART

Words and Music by
TYLER JOSEPH

Moderate Pop Rock

Ahn nyang ha se yo.

Some-times you got-ta bleed to
The songs on the ra - di - o are o - kay.

know
that you're a - live and have a soul.
But my taste in mu - sic is your face,

THE WALKER

Words and Music by MICHAEL FITZPATRICK,
JEREMY RUZUMNA, NOELLE SCAGGS,
JOSEPH KARNES, JAMES MIDHI KING
and JOHN MEREDITH WICKS

THINKING OUT LOUD

Words and Music by ED SHEERAN
and AMY WADGE

(La, la,   la,   la, la, la,   la, la, la,   la, la, la.)

D.S. al Coda

So, hon- ey, now, __

CODA

where we are.   Ba - by, we   found   love   right

where we are. _____   And we   found   love   right   where we   are. __

THE NEW DECADE SERIES

Books with Online Audio • Arranged for Piano, Voice, and Guitar

The New Decade Series features collections of iconic songs from each decade with great backing tracks so you can play them and sound like a pro. You access the tracks online for streaming or download. **See complete song listings online at www.halleonard.com**

SONGS OF THE 1920s

Ain't Misbehavin' • Baby Face • California, Here I Come • Fascinating Rhythm • I Wanna Be Loved by You • It Had to Be You • Mack the Knife • Ol' Man River • Puttin' on the Ritz • Rhapsody in Blue • Someone to Watch over Me • Tea for Two • Who's Sorry Now • and more.
00137576 P/V/G..................................$24.99

SONGS OF THE 1930s

As Time Goes By • Blue Moon • Cheek to Cheek • Embraceable You • A Fine Romance • Georgia on My Mind • I Only Have Eyes for You • The Lady Is a Tramp • On the Sunny Side of the Street • Over the Rainbow • Pennies from Heaven • Stormy Weather (Keeps Rainin' All the Time) • The Way You Look Tonight • and more.
00137579 P/V/G..................................$24.99

SONGS OF THE 1940s

At Last • Boogie Woogie Bugle Boy • Don't Get Around Much Anymore • God Bless' the Child • How High the Moon • It Could Happen to You • La Vie En Rose (Take Me to Your Heart Again) • Route 66 • Sentimental Journey • The Trolley Song • You'd Be So Nice to Come Home To • Zip-A-Dee-Doo-Dah • and more.
00137582 P/V/G..................................$24.99

SONGS OF THE 1950s

Ain't That a Shame • Be-Bop-A-Lula • Chantilly Lace • Earth Angel • Fever • Great Balls of Fire • Love Me Tender • Mona Lisa • Peggy Sue • Que Sera, Sera (Whatever Will Be, Will Be) • Rock Around the Clock • Sixteen Tons • A Teenager in Love • That'll Be the Day • Unchained Melody • Volare • You Send Me • Your Cheatin' Heart • and more.
00137595 P/V/G..................................$24.99

SONGS OF THE 1960s

All You Need Is Love • Beyond the Sea • Born to Be Wild • California Girls • Dancing in the Street • Happy Together • King of the Road • Leaving on a Jet Plane • Louie, Louie • My Generation • Oh, Pretty Woman • Sunshine of Your Love • Under the Boardwalk • You Really Got Me • and more.
00137596 P/V/G $24.99

SONGS OF THE 1970s

ABC • Bridge over Troubled Water • Cat's in the Cradle • Dancing Queen • Free Bird • Goodbye Yellow Brick Road • Hotel California • I Will Survive • Joy to the World • Killing Me Softly with His Song • Layla • Let It Be • Piano Man • The Rainbow Connection • Stairway to Heaven • The Way We Were • Your Song • and more.
00137599 P/V/G $27.99

SONGS OF THE 1980s

Addicted to Love • Beat It • Careless Whisper • Come on Eileen • Don't Stop Believin' • Every Rose Has Its Thorn • Footloose • I Just Called to Say I Love You • Jessie's Girl • Livin' on a Prayer • Saving All My Love for You • Take on Me • Up Where We Belong • The Wind Beneath My Wings • and more.
00137600 P/V/G $27.99

SONGS OF THE 1990s

Angel • Black Velvet • Can You Feel the Love Tonight • (Everything I Do) I Do It for You • Friends in Low Places • Hero • I Will Always Love You • More Than Words • My Heart Will Go On (Love Theme from 'Titanic') • Smells like Teen Spirit • Under the Bridge • Vision of Love • Wonderwall • and more.
00137601 P/V/G $27.99

SONGS OF THE 2000s

Bad Day • Beautiful • Before He Cheats • Chasing Cars • Chasing Pavements • Drops of Jupiter (Tell Me) • Fireflies • Hey There Delilah • How to Save a Life • I Gotta Feeling • I'm Yours • Just Dance • Love Story • 100 Years • Rehab • Unwritten • You Raise Me Up • and more.
00137608 P/V/G..................................$27.99

SONGS OF THE 2010S

All About That Bass • All of Me • Brave • Empire State of Mind • Get Lucky • Happy • Hey, Soul Sister • I Knew You Were Trouble • Just the Way You Are • Need You Now • Pompeii • Radioactive • Rolling in the Deep • Shake It Off • Shut up and Dance • Stay with Me • Take Me to Church • Thinking Out Loud • Uptown Funk • and many more.
00151836 P/V/G $27.99

HAL•LEONARD®
CORPORATION

7777 W. BLUEMOUND RD. P.O. BOX 13819 MILWAUKEE, WI 53213

halleonard.com

Prices, content, and availability subject to change without notice.

0516

THE BEST EVER
COLLECTION
ARRANGED FOR PIANO, VOICE AND GUITAR

100 of the Most Beautiful Piano Solos Ever
100 songs
00102787 ....$27.50

150 of the Most Beautiful Songs Ever
150 ballads
00360735 ....$27.00

More of the Best Acoustic Rock Songs Ever
69 tunes
00311738 ....$19.95

Best Acoustic Rock Songs Ever
65 acoustic hits
00310984 ....$19.95

Best Big Band Songs Ever
68 big band hits
00359129 ....$17.99

Best Blues Songs Ever
73 blues tunes
00312874 ....$19.99

Best Broadway Songs Ever
83 songs
00309155 ....$24.99

More of the Best Broadway Songs Ever
82 songs
00311501 ....$22.95

Best Children's Songs Ever
101 songs
00159272 ....$19.99

Best Christmas Songs Ever
69 holiday favorites
00359130 ....$24.99

Best Classic Rock Songs Ever
64 hits
00310800 ....$22.99

Best Classical Music Ever
86 classical favorites
00310674 (Piano Solo) $19.95

The Best Country Rock Songs Ever
52 hits
00118881 ....$19.99

Best Country Songs Ever
78 classic country hits
00359135 ....$19.99

Best Disco Songs Ever
50 songs
00312565 ....$19.99

Best Dixieland Songs Ever
90 songs
00312326 ....$19.99

Best Early Rock 'n' Roll Songs Ever
74 songs
00310816 ....$19.95

Best Easy Listening Songs Ever
75 mellow favorites
00359193 ....$19.99

Best Folk/Pop Songs Ever
66 hits
00138299 ....$19.99

Best Gospel Songs Ever
80 gospel songs
00310503 ....$19.99

Best Hymns Ever
118 hymns
00310774 ....$18.99

Best Jazz Piano Solos Ever
80 songs
00312079 ....$19.99

Best Jazz Standards Ever
77 jazz hits
00311641 ....$19.95

More of the Best Jazz Standards Ever
74 beloved jazz hits
00311023 ....$19.95

Best Latin Songs Ever
67 songs
00310355 ....$19.99

HAL•LEONARD®
Visit us online
for complete songlists at
www.halleonard.com

Prices, contents and availability subject to change without
notice. Not all products available outside the U.S.A.

Best Love Songs Ever
62 favorite love songs
00359198 ....$19.99

Best Movie Songs Ever
71 songs
00310063 ....$19.99

Best Movie Soundtrack Songs Ever
70 songs
00146161 ....$16.99

Best Pop/Rock Songs Ever
50 classics
00138279 ....$19.99

Best Praise & Worship Songs Ever
80 all-time favorites
00311057 ....$22.99

More of the Best Praise & Worship Songs Ever
76 songs
00311800 ....$24.99

Best R&B Songs Ever
66 songs
00310184 ....$19.95

Best Rock Songs Ever
63 songs
00490424 ....$18.95

Best Showtunes Ever
71 songs
00118782 ....$19.99

Best Songs Ever
72 must-own classics
00359224 ....$24.99

Best Soul Songs Ever
70 hits
00311427 ....$19.95

Best Standards Ever, Vol. 1 (A-L)
72 beautiful ballads
00359231 ....$17.95

Best Standards Ever, Vol. 2 (M-Z)
73 songs
00359232 ....$17.99

Best Torch Songs Ever
70 sad and sultry favorites
00311027 ....$19.95

Best Wedding Songs Ever
70 songs
00311096 ....$19.95

0916

BIG BOOKS of Music

Our "Big Books" feature big selections of popular titles under one cover, perfect for performing musicians, music aficionados or the serious hobbyist. All books are arranged for piano, voice, and guitar, and feature stay-open binding, so the books lie flat without breaking the spine.

    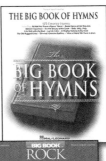 

BIG BOOK OF BALLADS – 2ND ED.
62 songs.
00310485 .... $19.95

BIG BOOK OF BIG BAND HITS
84 songs.
00310701 .... $22.99

BIG BOOK OF BLUEGRASS SONGS
70 songs.
00311484 .... $19.95

BIG BOOK OF BLUES
80 songs.
00311843 .... $19.99

BIG BOOK OF BROADWAY
70 songs.
00311658 .... $19.95

BIG BOOK OF CHILDREN'S SONGS
55 songs.
00359261 .... $16.99

GREAT BIG BOOK OF CHILDREN'S SONGS
76 songs.
00310002 .... $15.99

FANTASTIC BIG BOOK OF CHILDREN'S SONGS
66 songs.
00311062 .... $17.95

BIG BOOK OF CHRISTMAS SONGS – 2ND ED.
126 songs.
00311520 .... $19.95

BIG BOOK OF CLASSICAL MUSIC
100 songs.
00310508 .... $19.99

BIG BOOK OF CONTEMPORARY CHRISTIAN FAVORITES – 3RD ED.
50 songs.
00312067 .... $21.99

BIG BOOK OF '50s & '60s SWINGING SONGS
67 songs.
00310982 .... $19.95

BIG BOOK OF FOLKSONGS
125 songs.
00312549 .... $19.99

BIG BOOK OF FRENCH SONGS
70 songs.
00311154 .... $19.95

BIG BOOK OF GERMAN SONGS
78 songs.
00311816 .... $19.99

BIG BOOK OF GOSPEL SONGS
100 songs.
00310604 .... $19.95

BIG BOOK OF HYMNS
125 hymns.
00310510 .... $17.95

BIG BOOK OF IRISH SONGS
76 songs.
00310981 .... $19.95

BIG BOOK OF ITALIAN FAVORITES
80 songs.
00311185 .... $19.99

BIG BOOK OF JAZZ – 2ND ED.
75 songs.
00311557 .... $19.95

BIG BOOK OF LATIN AMERICAN SONGS
89 songs.
00311562 .... $19.95

BIG BOOK OF LOVE SONGS
80 songs.
00310784 .... $19.95

BIG BOOK OF MOTOWN
84 songs.
00311061 .... $19.95

BIG BOOK OF MOVIE MUSIC
72 songs.
00311582 .... $19.95

BIG BOOK OF NOSTALGIA
158 songs.
00310004 .... $24.99

BIG BOOK OF OLDIES
73 songs.
00310756 .... $19.95

THE BIG BOOK OF PRAISE & WORSHIP
52 songs.
00140795 .... $22.99

BIG BOOK OF RAGTIME PIANO
63 songs.
00311749 .... $19.95

BIG BOOK OF ROCK
78 songs.
00311566 .... $22.95

BIG BOOK OF SOUL
71 songs.
00310771 .... $19.95

BIG BOOK OF STANDARDS
86 songs.
00311667 .... $19.95

BIG BOOK OF SWING
84 songs.
00310359 .... $19.95

BIG BOOK OF TORCH SONGS – 2ND ED.
75 songs.
00310561 .... $19.99

BIG BOOK OF TV THEME SONGS
78 songs.
00310504 .... $19.95

BIG BOOK OF WEDDING MUSIC
77 songs.
00311567 .... $19.95

Prices, contents, and availability subject to change without notice.

Visit **www.halleonard.com**
for our entire catalog and to view our complete songlists.

THE GRAMMY AWARDS

SONGBOOKS FROM HAL LEONARD

These elite collections of the nominees and winners of Grammy Awards since the honor's inception in 1958 provide a snapshot of the changing times in popular music.

PIANO/VOCAL/GUITAR

GRAMMY AWARDS RECORD OF THE YEAR 1958–2011

Beat It • Beautiful Day • Bridge over Troubled Water • Don't Know Why • Don't Worry, Be Happy • The Girl from Ipanema (Garôta De Ipanema) • Hotel California • I Will Always Love You • Just the Way You Are • Mack the Knife • Moon River • My Heart Will Go on (Love Theme from 'Titanic') • Rehab • Sailing • Unforgettable • Up, Up and Away • The Wind Beneath My Wings • and more.
00313603 P/V/G.................... $19.99

THE GRAMMY AWARDS SONG OF THE YEAR 1958–1969

Battle of New Orleans • Born Free • Fever • The Good Life • A Hard Day's Night • Harper Valley P.T.A. • Hello, Dolly! • Hey Jude • King of the Road • Little Green Apples • Mrs. Robinson • Ode to Billy Joe • People • Somewhere, My Love • Strangers in the Night • A Time for Us (Love Theme) • Volare • Witchcraft • Yesterday • and more.
00313598 P/V/G.................... $19.99

THE GRAMMY AWARDS SONG OF THE YEAR 1970–1979

Alone Again (Naturally) • American Pie • At Seventeen • Don't It Make My Brown Eyes Blue • Honesty • (I Never Promised You A) Rose Garden • I Write the Songs • Killing Me Softly with His Song • Let It Be • Me and Bobby McGee • Send in the Clowns • Song Sung Blue • Stayin' Alive • Three Times a Lady • The Way We Were • You're So Vain • You've Got a Friend • and more.
00313599 P/V/G.................... $19.99

THE GRAMMY AWARDS SONG OF THE YEAR 1980–1989

Against All Odds (Take a Look at Me Now) • Always on My Mind • Beat It • Bette Davis Eyes • Don't Worry, Be Happy • Ebony and Ivory • Endless Love • Every Breath You Take • Eye of the Tiger • Fame • Fast Car • Hello • I Just Called to Say I Love You • La Bamba • Nine to Five • The Rose • Somewhere Out There • Time After Time • We Are the World • and more.
00313600 P/V/G.................... $19.99

THE GRAMMY AWARDS SONG OF THE YEAR 1990–1999

Can You Feel the Love Tonight • (Everything I Do) I Do It for You • From a Distance • Give Me One Reason • I Swear • Kiss from a Rose • Losing My Religion • My Heart Will Go on (Love Theme from 'Titanic') • Nothing Compares 2 U • Smooth • Streets of Philadelphia • Tears in Heaven • Unforgettable • Walking in Memphis • A Whole New World • You Oughta Know • and more.
00313601 P/V/G.................... $19.99

THE GRAMMY AWARDS SONG OF THE YEAR 2000–2009

Beautiful • Beautiful Day • Breathe • Chasing Pavements • Complicated • Dance with My Father • Daughters • Don't Know Why • Fallin' • I Hope You Dance • I'm Yours • Live like You Were Dying • Poker Face • Rehab • Single Ladies (Put a Ring on It) • A Thousand Miles • Umbrella • Use Somebody • Viva La Vida • and more.
00313602 P/V/G.................... $19.99

THE GRAMMY AWARDS BEST COUNTRY SONG 1964–2011

Always on My Mind • Before He Cheats • Behind Closed Doors • Bless the Broken Road • Butterfly Kisses • Dang Me • Forever and Ever, Amen • The Gambler • I Still Believe in You • I Swear • King of the Road • Live like You Were Dying • Love Can Build a Bridge • Need You Now • On the Road Again • White Horse • You Decorated My Life • and more.
00313604 P/V/G.................... $19.99

THE GRAMMY AWARDS BEST R&B SONG 1958–2011

After the Love Has Gone • Ain't No Sunshine • Be Without You • Billie Jean • End of the Road • Good Golly Miss Molly • Hit the Road Jack • If You Don't Know Me by Now • Papa's Got a Brand New Bag • Respect • Shine • Single Ladies (Put a Ring on It) • (Sittin' On) the Dock of the Bay • Superstition • U Can't Touch This • We Belong Together • and more.
00313605 P/V/G.................... $19.99

THE GRAMMY AWARDS BEST POP & ROCK GOSPEL ALBUMS (2000–2011)

Call My Name • Come on Back to Me • Deeper Walk • Forever • Gone • I Need You • I Smile • I Will Follow • King • Leaving 99 • Lifesong • Looking Back at You • Much of You • My Love Remains • Say So • Somebody's Watching • Step by Step/Forever We Will Sing • Tunnel • Unforgetful You • You Hold My World • Your Love Is a Song • and more.
00313680 P/V/G.................... $16.99

ELECTRONIC KEYBOARD

THE GRAMMY AWARDS RECORD OF THE YEAR 1958-2011 – VOL. 160

All I Wanna Do • Bridge over Troubled Water • Don't Know Why • The Girl from Ipanema (Garôta De Ipanema) • Hotel California • I Will Always Love You • Just the Way You Are • Killing Me Softly with His Song • Love Will Keep Us Together • Rehab • Unforgettable • What's Love Got to Do with It • The Wind Beneath My Wings • and more.
00100315 E-Z Play Today #160 .... $16.99

PRO VOCAL

WOMEN'S EDITIONS

THE GRAMMY AWARDS BEST FEMALE POP VOCAL PERFORMANCE 1990-1999 — VOL. 57

Book/CD Pack

All I Wanna Do • Building a Mystery • Constant Craving • I Will Always Love You • I Will Remember You • My Heart Will Go on (Love Theme from 'Titanic') • No More "I Love You's" • Something to Talk About (Let's Give Them Something to Talk About) • Unbreak My Heart • Vision of Love.
00740446 Melody/Lyrics/Chords................. $14.99

THE GRAMMY AWARDS BEST FEMALE POP VOCAL PERFORMANCE 2000-2009 – VOL. 58

Book/CD Pack

Ain't No Other Man • Beautiful • Chasing Pavements • Don't Know Why • Halo • I Try • I'm like a Bird • Rehab • Since U Been Gone • Sunrise.
00740447 Melody/Lyrics/Chords................. $14.99

MEN'S EDITIONS

THE GRAMMY AWARDS BEST MALE POP VOCAL PERFORMANCE 1990-1999 – VOL. 59

Book/CD Pack

Brand New Day • Can You Feel the Love Tonight • Candle in the Wind 1997 • Change the World • If I Ever Lose My Faith in You • Kiss from a Rose • My Father's Eyes • Oh, Pretty Woman • Tears in Heaven • When a Man Loves a Woman.
00740448 Melody/Lyrics/Chords................. $14.99

THE GRAMMY AWARDS BEST MALE POP VOCAL PERFORMANCE 2000-2009 – VOL. 60

Book/CD Pack

Cry Me a River • Daughters • Don't Let Me Be Lonely Tonight • Make It Mine • Say • Waiting on the World to Change • What Goes Around...Comes Around Interlude • Your Body Is a Wonderland.
00740449 Melody/Lyrics/Chords................. $14.99

Prices, contents, and availabilbility subject to change without notice.

HAL•LEONARD® CORPORATION

7777 W. BLUEMOUND RD. P.O. BOX 13819 MILWAUKEE, WI 53213

www.halleonard.com

0713